KU-211-594

I am big.

I am bigger than you are.

The Best Bug Parade

I am the biggest bug by far.

Bug Parade

Big. Bigger! Biggest!!

I am small.

I am smaller than small.

I am the smallest bug of them all.

Small.   Smaller!   Smallest!!

I am long.

Bug Parade

I am longer than you.

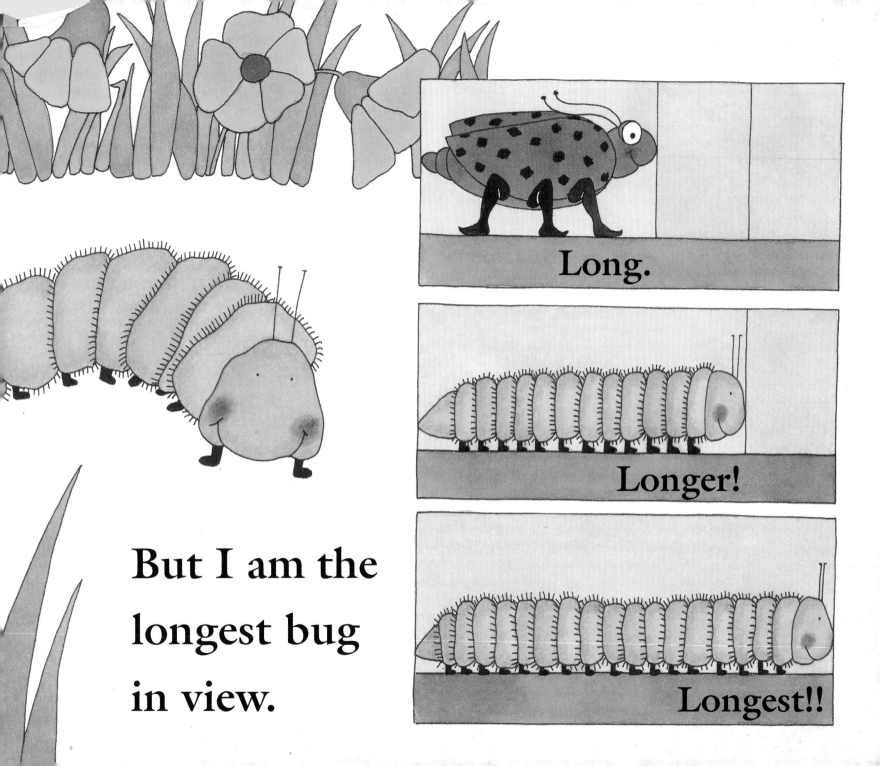

Long.

Longer!

But I am the longest bug in view.

Longest!!

I am short.

I am shorter than short.

I am the shortest bug of this sort.

Short.

Shorter!

Shortest!!

When we are all together,
long and short, big and small,

we are not just good or better,

we are . . .

The Best Bug Parade of All!

Bug Parade

ACTIVITIES AT SCHOOL

The following activities will help you to extend children's understanding of the concepts presented in *The Best Bug Parade*:

- Read the story with the children and ask them to describe what is going on in each picture. Ask questions throughout the story, such as 'Do the bugs look the same or do they look different?' and 'How do they look different?'

- Ask the children to draw and colour some of their own imaginary bugs. Cut them out and help the children arrange them in order of size. The class can then line up their bugs for their own best bug parade.

- Use the vocabulary 'long, longer, longest' and 'short, shorter, shortest' to discuss the distance a ball or beanbag is kicked or thrown. Measure each distance using suitable standard or uniform non-standard units to prove which is longer, shortest, etc.

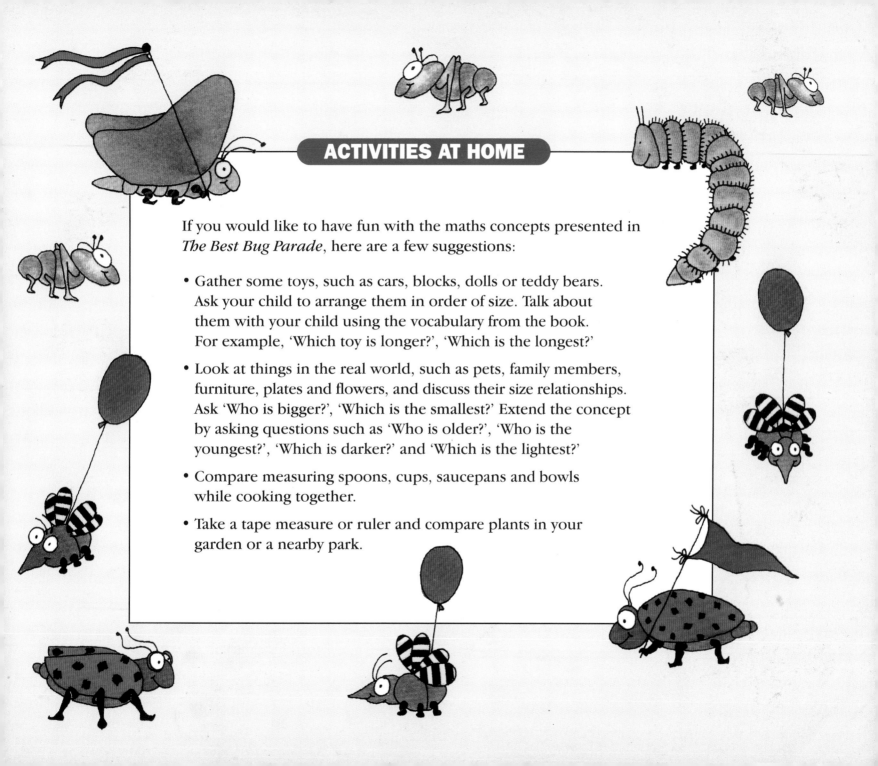

ACTIVITIES AT HOME

If you would like to have fun with the maths concepts presented in *The Best Bug Parade*, here are a few suggestions:

• Gather some toys, such as cars, blocks, dolls or teddy bears. Ask your child to arrange them in order of size. Talk about them with your child using the vocabulary from the book. For example, 'Which toy is longer?', 'Which is the longest?'

• Look at things in the real world, such as pets, family members, furniture, plates and flowers, and discuss their size relationships. Ask 'Who is bigger?', 'Which is the smallest?' Extend the concept by asking questions such as 'Who is older?', 'Who is the youngest?', 'Which is darker?' and 'Which is the lightest?'

• Compare measuring spoons, cups, saucepans and bowls while cooking together.

• Take a tape measure or ruler and compare plants in your garden or a nearby park.